B·E·S·T
Friends

Written by Cass Hollander ▪ Illustrated by Ann Barrow

MODERN CURRICULUM PRESS

PROJECT DIRECTOR: **Judith E. Nayer**
ART DIRECTOR: **Lisa Lopez**

Published by Modern Curriculum Press

 Modern Curriculum Press, Inc.
A division of Simon & Schuster
13900 Prospect Road, Cleveland, Ohio 44136

This edition is published simultaneously in Canada by
Globe/Modern Curriculum Press, Toronto.

ISBN 0-8136-1105-9 (STY PK)   ISBN 0-8136-1102-4 (BK)

10 9 8 7 6 5 4 3 2   95 94 93 92

When you find
something special,
like a genuine arrowhead,

and you want to tell
someone all about it,
who do you tell?

Your best friend

When you enter
your pet in a contest,
and the judges say he's the best,

and you want to tell
someone all about it,
who do you tell?

4

Your best friend

When you go to a museum,
and see a stegosaurus skeleton,

and you want to tell
someone all about it,
who do you tell?

Your best friend

When you've had a terrible day,
and you get home tired and upset,

and you want to tell
someone all about it,
who do you tell?

Your best friend

When you guess
how many jelly beans,
and it turns out
your guess is correct,

and you want to tell
someone all about it,
who do you tell?

Your best friend

When you see a yellow flower
growing through a crack
in the cement,

and you want to tell
someone all about it,
who do you tell?

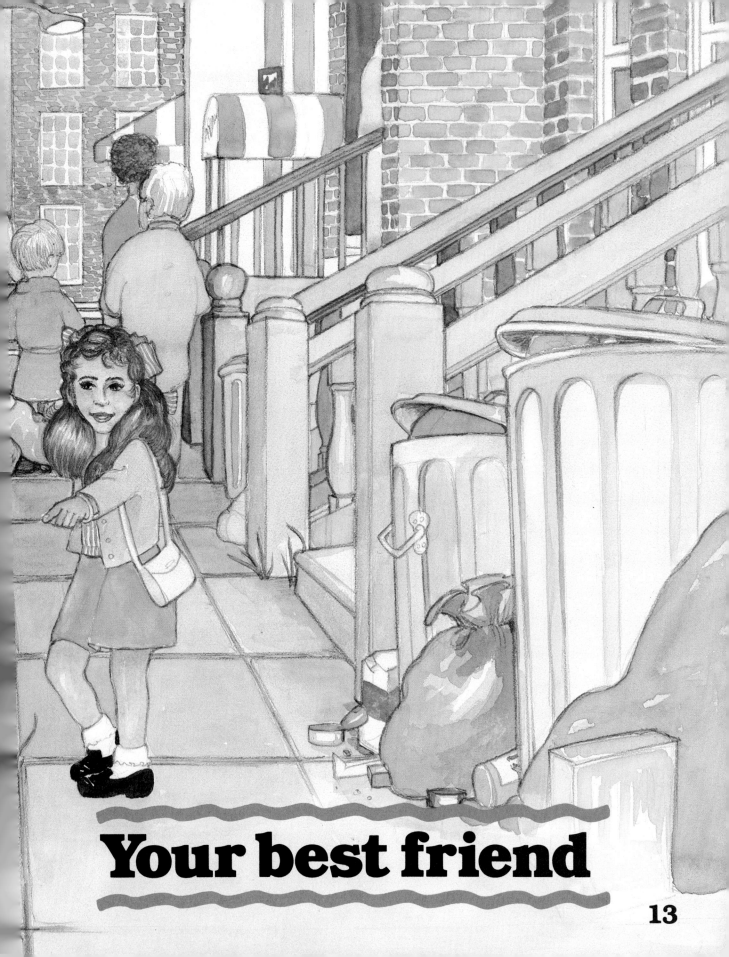

Your best friend

When you're all set to fall asleep,
but you think something's
under the bed,

and you want to tell
someone all about it,
who do you tell?

Your best friend